Gardens and Parks

Správa Pražského hradu

Prague Castle

Gardens and Parks

© Prague Castle Administration *(Správa Pražského hradu)*, 2002
Text © Věra Vávrová, 2002
English translation © Alastair Millar, 2002
Photography © Zdeněk Thoma, 2002
Maps © Vojtěch Veverka, 2002
Graphic design © Ivan Exner, 2002

ISBN 80-86 161-63-3

◀ *Part of the Hartig Garden beneath the Little Look-out*

St Vitus' Cathedral and the Powder Tower from the Royal Garden

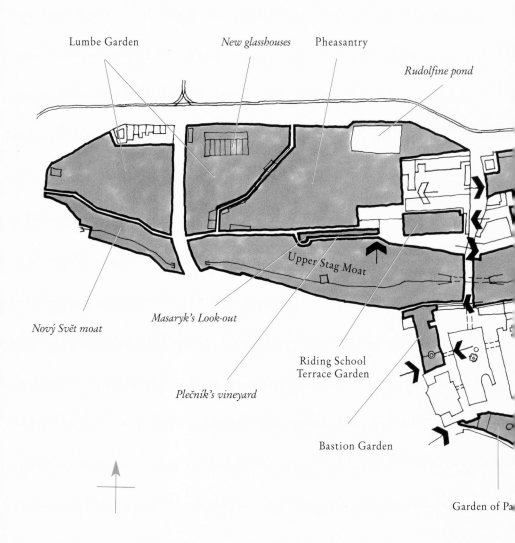

Lumbe Garden

New glasshouses

Pheasantry

Rudolfine pond

Nový Svět moat

Masaryk's Look-out

Upper Stag Moat

Plečník's vineyard

Riding School
Terrace Garden

Bastion Garden

Garden of Pa

0   50   100   150 m

GARDENS AND PARKS OF PRAGUE CASTLE

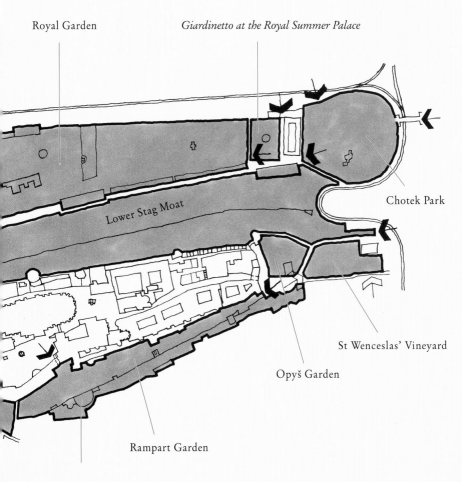

Royal Garden

Giardinetto at the Royal Summer Palace

Lower Stag Moat

Chotek Park

St Wenceslas' Vineyard

Opyš Garden

Rampart Garden

adise   Hartig Garden

A band of green surrounds the rocky promontory on which,
sometime around the end of the 9th century AD,
the Bohemian Princes founded their seat. Trees and bushes
previously grew on its slopes, but as the centuries passed
the sovereigns' residence grew into the majestic form
of Prague Castle today and the greenery around
it also changed – vineyards and gardens sprang up,
some of which retained a woodland aspect.
Grapevines were first to be cultivated on the hillsides around
the castle. A vineyard was founded on the site of what is now
St Wenceslas' Vineyard *(Svatováclavská vinice)*
on the slope beneath Opyš in 1375. At this time, herbs
and fruit were grown in gardens primarily for those dwelling
in monastic houses – the nuns of St George's Convent,
too, had their own garden and vinery. Of the gardens
of the Royal Court in the Early Middle Ages, however,
no report has come down to us. The first formal garden
at Prague Castle – the Royal Garden *(Královská zahrada)* –
was established by Ferdinand I in 1534;
he selected the site for it, north of the steep cleft
of the Brusnice stream. Work on the Royal Garden
was continued by Ferdinand of the Tyrol,
and the Emperors Maximilian I and Rudolf II, as well as
other monarchs, also cared for it.
Ferdinand of the Tyrol established his own private garden
on the southern slopes beneath the Castle in 1557 – this was
the first garden on the site of what is now the Garden
of Paradise *(Rajská zahrada)*. The present

Chotek Park *(Chotkovy sady)* adjoins the Royal Garden, and during the Renaissance was the setting for various amusements and tournaments. From the 17th century onwards the area began to be used for more practical purposes, and later the first public park in Prague appeared here. The land of what is now the Lower Stag Moat *(Dolní Jelení příkop)* was in large part purchased by Ferdinand I when the Royal Garden was founded. Almost all of the Upper Stag Moat *(Horní Jelení příkop)* and part of the Lower was later bought by Emperor Rudolf II, who had game introduced here. Rudolf II also founded the Pheasantry *(Bažantnice)* west of what is now the Riding School. When in 1918 Tomáš Garrigue Masaryk selected Prague Castle as the seat of government after the creation of Czechoslovakia, he decided to return this ancient place its stately aspect, and emphasise its importance and grandeur. He paid great attention not only to the buildings themselves, but also to the courts and gardens. As early as 1920 renovations began of the area along the southern facade of the castle, where the Garden of Paradise (on the site of what had once been Ferdinand of the Tyrol's garden) and the Rampart Garden *(zahrada Na Valech)* were founded. In 1925 the Office of the President of the Republic purchased the so-called Lumbe Garden *(Lumbeho zahrada)* northwest of the Castle. A unique garden reminiscent of those in Japan and Italy was founded in 1932 is the area of the former bastion yard – the Bastion Garden *(zahrada Na Baště)*.

In the 1950's the Riding School Terrace Garden was created
on the roof of the garages then built there, on the site
of the former Summer Riding School. The Palace
Hartig Garden *(Hartigovská zahrada)* was incorporated
into Prague Castle in the 1960's, although its origins lie
in the 17th century. In all, greenery covers some 34 ha today.
The following pages present a journey around
Prague Castle, through the whole circuit of its gardens
and parks, beginning with six gardens – the Royal,
Riding School Terrace, Bastion, Paradise, Hartig
and Rampart. These are carefully cultivated and maintained
by the gardeners so that in visiting them one can wonder
at the composition of the trees, bushes and flowers
as well as the unique buildings and other monuments
of various centuries. In the summer season all
of the gardens are open to the public at regular hours.
The former Pheasantry and part of the Lumbe Garden
serve a practical purpose. After reconstruction,
St Wenceslas' Vineyard too will be used for growing
grapevines and fruit trees. At the present time these areas
are not open to the public, but their future renovation
and further use is planned. Finally, the Stag Moat
and Chotek Park represent an isolated phenomenon within
the metropolis – in the immediate vicinity of the unique
Castle complex it is possible to wander among
the trees, listen to birdsong and watch the play of the water.
A similarly harmonious ensemble is to be found
nowhere else in the world.

11

The walks through each garden, with descriptions
of their individual features, plants and points
of interest are complemented by an overview of their histories.
Various events and the work of those who contributed
to the creation and cultivation of the gardens are recalled.
Former Director of the Castle Gardens Jan Ondřej,
in his book *Zahrady Pražského hradu* ('The Gardens of Prague
Castle') wrote that they should be appreciated thus:
"Ceaseless change is the basic quality of the garden,
as it is for nature as a whole. Unlike buildings, fountains
and statues the garden remains an ever-unfinished work.
The garden artist, creating his picture of nature as does
a painter, albeit with plants, must consider how
it will appear later, both in which season and after years
as it matures. He must see at least a century ahead... he must
acclimatise to the plants, in order that he knows what
they need and where to place them. And it takes
years before the garden, in a word, grows into the vision
of its creator, and only then on the condition
that for the whole period he has conserved and cared
for his thought... As without the presence of Man,
the creator of the garden and the generations
of generally nameless individuals – the gardener
and his assistants – no shaped garden space
could come to be or be... And if all succeeds, and not
only from plants, but also from paths, steps, pergolas,
statuary, buildings etc. an artwork is created, then we can
step into a garden as into an art gallery.
And wonder at its beauty...".

I. THE ROYAL GARDEN

The jewel among the gardens of Prague Castle is the Royal Garden. For centuries it was a closed space next to the seat of the sovereign or, later, the President of the Republic. Every age has left its mark on the garden – with an original Renaissance design reminiscent of

13

a *giardinetto*, the Baroque echoes of the parterres with their floral ornament, and the trees and bushes growing freely in the grass in the manner of a landscaped English park. The unusual views of Prague Castle from the north enhance the attractiveness of a walk here. Prior to November 1989 the Royal Garden was opened only exceptionally, and even then visitors were allowed only in the gardens around the Royal Summer Palace, divided off by iron railings. At Easter 1990, after a decision by President Václav Havel,

The lower parterre with fountain and floral beds

the garden was opened to the public and began to reveal its secrets. It can now be visited during the summer season at regular opening hours.

Walk

The Royal Gardens may be entered either from next to the Royal Summer Palace or through the decorative grilled gate from ul. U Prašného mostu. From the gate leads a short avenue of white and red flowering chestnuts, pruned to shape every second year.

To the left is the Lion Court with its Renaissance facade facing onto the garden; it was previously known as the Bear Court. Its origins reach back as far as the founder of the Royal Garden, Ferdinand I. Originally a wooden menagerie stood nearby, which under Rudolf II

Flowering cherry near the Ball Court, now replaced by a younger tree

15

was replaced by a stone structure that over the centuries was renovated several times. In the 1960's the building served as a restaurant. The most recent reconstruction was undertaken in 1994–5 to designs by the architect Josef Pleskot. Archive records

The new glasshouse in the western part of the Orangery
Rose beds in front of the "Empire style" glasshouse / The southern facade of the Garden Residence

show that, in turn, tigers, lions, wildcats, leopards, wolves, lynxes, foxes and also birds of prey were bred in the Lion Court. The best known of the lions was Mohamed, a gift to Emperor Rudolf II from the Turkish Sultan. According to the astrologer Tycho Brahe it was to meet the same fate as the Emperor himself, and for this reason the latter took great pains over its welfare. The last animal to reside in the Lion Court was a bear mentioned in 1740, when it was sent to Count Thun in Děčín. Bears were still to be found in the Royal Garden in 1920; prior to the building of the bear pit in the Stag Moat they were temporarily housed in the Fig House.

In the summer palms are displayed behind the low, decorative wall to the left of the garden entrance, and beyond these is a pleasant view of the Rose Garden. Close by stands an 1820 glasshouse in which the plants used to decorate the reception rooms and exteriors of Prague Castle are grown.

To the right of the entrance path is a carefully cultivated grassy parterre with ornamental flower-beds, stretching to the Garden Residence building in which until 1950 several presidents lived. Originally a glasshouse built to a design by the Court Master Builder Kilián Ignác Dientzenhofer in 1730–31 stood here. As early as 1757 this was almost completely razed by the Prussians, and at the end of the 18th century its central section was converted into a small belvedere on a design by the Court Master Builder Antonín Haffenecker. After the creation of the Czechoslovak Republic it was used occasionally by President Tomáš Garrigue Masaryk and his daughter Alice. A fundamental renovation into a residence for the President of the Republic was proposed by Castle Architect Pavel Janák in 1946–47; in view of the changes in political development its first user as such was Klement Gottwald in 1950. Close to the residence grow groups of coniferous and evergreen broad-leaved trees such as dawn redwoods (metasequoias) and eastern (Canadian) hemlock. The route continues down between balustrades bearing Baroque putti playing with lions by Matyáš Bernard Braun. On the

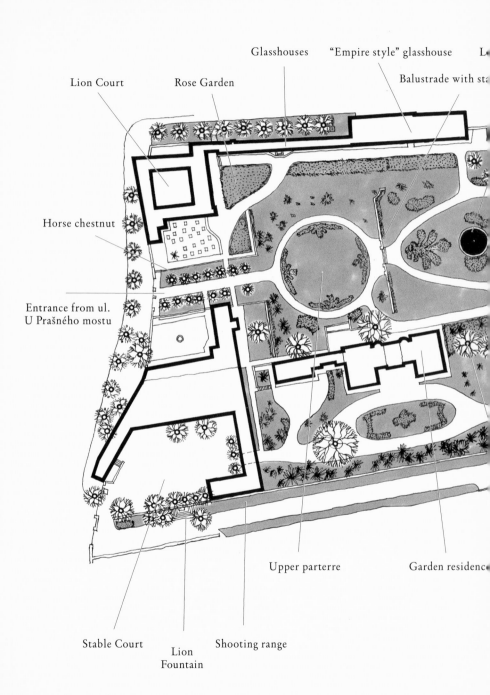

Glasshouses   "Empire style" glasshouse   L◦

Lion Court   Rose Garden

Balustrade with st◦

Horse chestnut

Entrance from ul.
U Prašného mostu

Upper parterre   Garden residenc◦

Stable Court   Shooting range

Lion
Fountain

THE GIARDINETTO BY THE ROYAL SUMMER PALACE

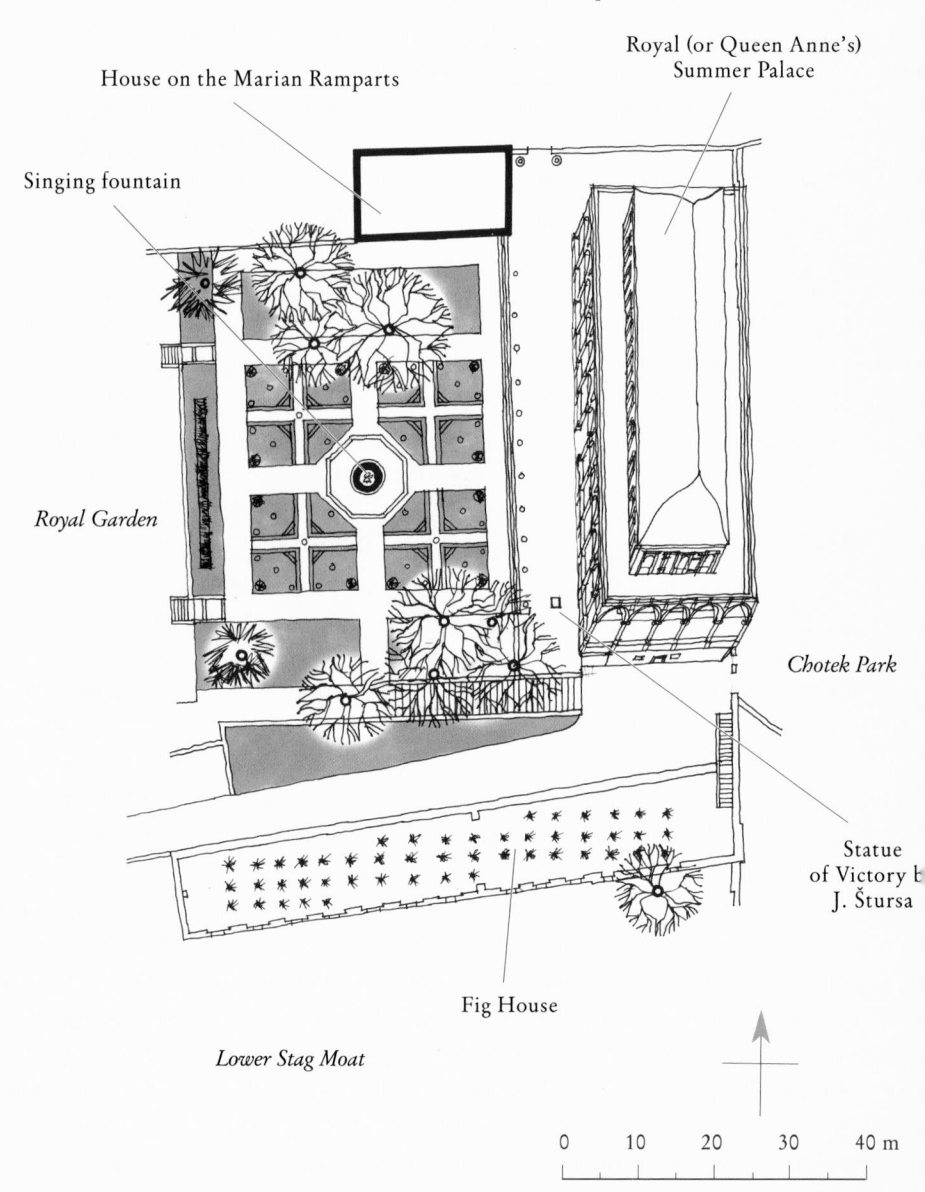

Marian Ramparts

Royal (or Queen Anne's)
Summer Palace

House on the Marian Ramparts

Singing fountain

Royal Garden

Chotek Park

Statue
of Victory b
J. Štursa

Fig House

Lower Stag Moat

0   10   20   30   40 m

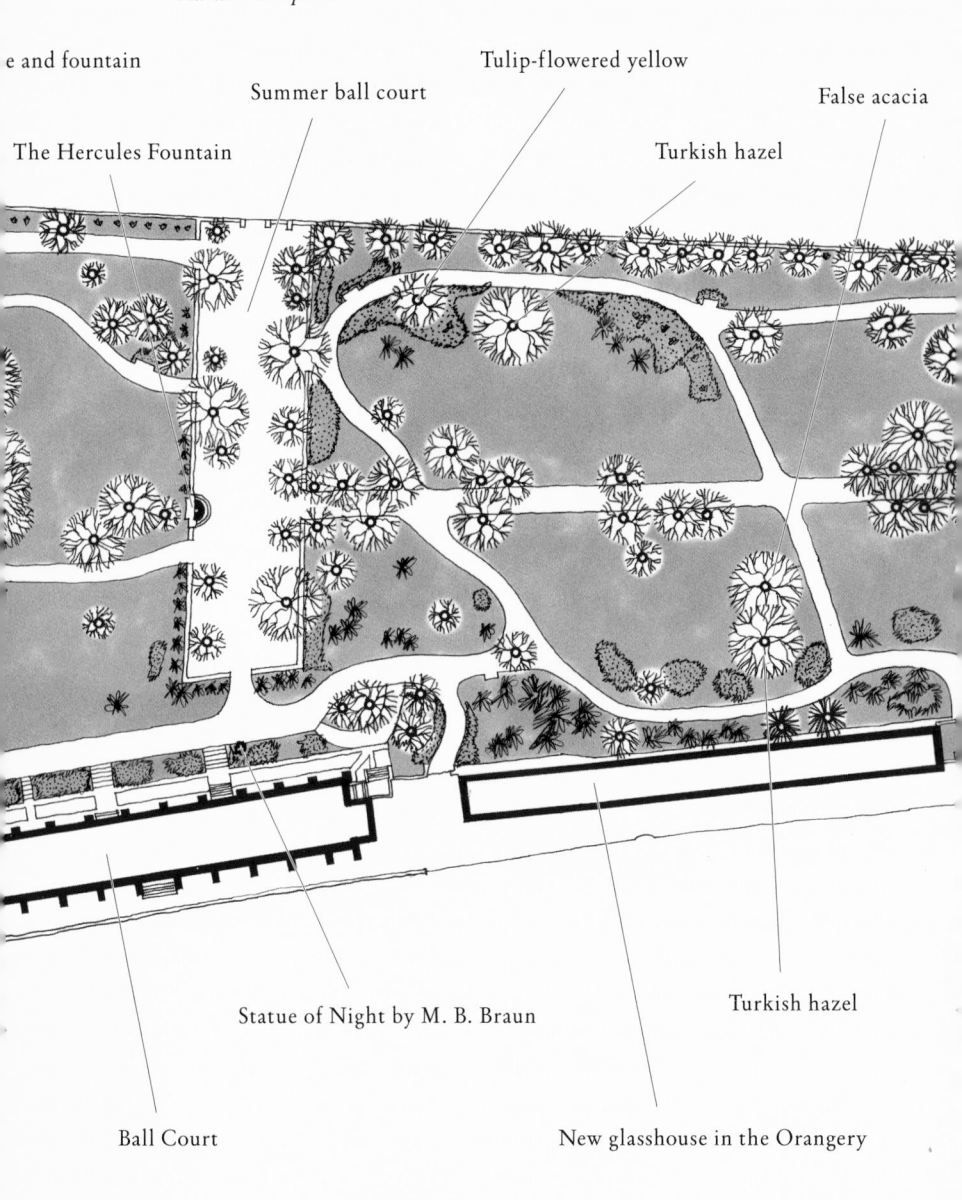

Marian Ramparts

e and fountain

Tulip-flowered yellow

Summer ball court

False acacia

The Hercules Fountain

Turkish hazel

Statue of Night by M. B. Braun

Turkish hazel

Ball Court

New glasshouse in the Orangery

Lower Stag Moat

THE ROYAL GARDEN

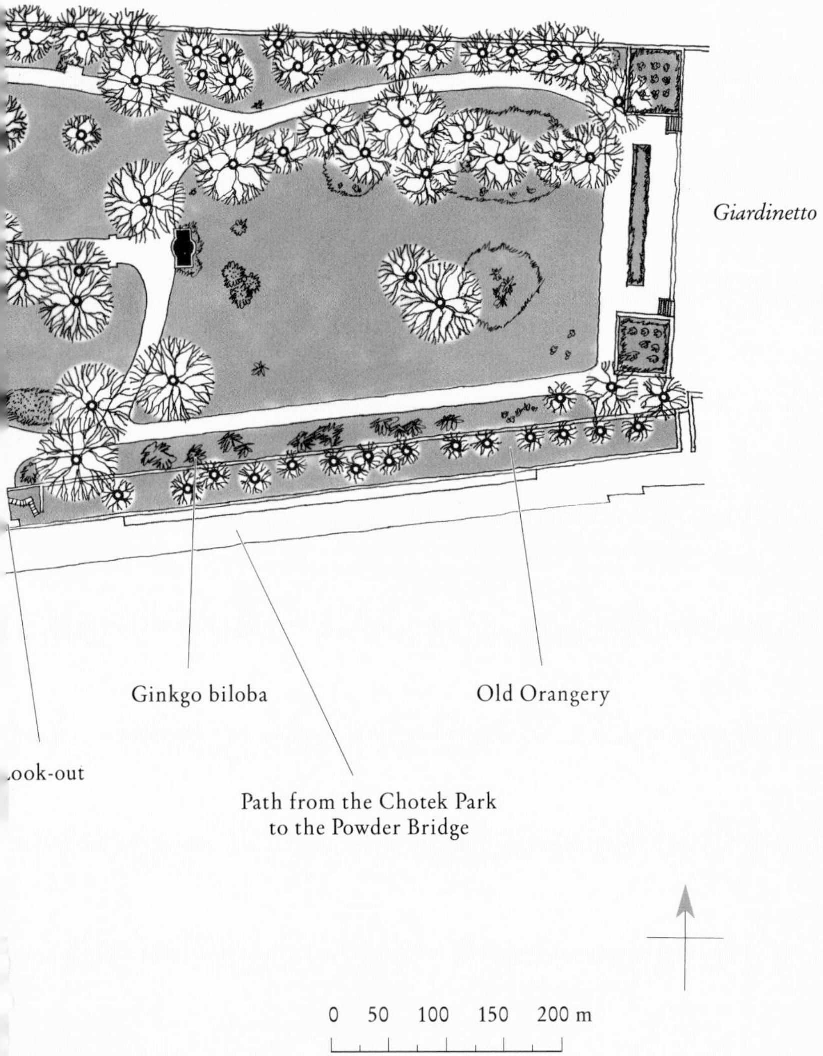

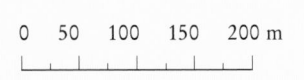

Giardinetto

Ginkgo biloba

Old Orangery

Look-out

Path from the Chotek Park
to the Powder Bridge

0   50   100   150   200 m

The Singing Fountain

right side the 1730 original was replaced in 1953 with a copy by the sculptor Josef Wagner. The steps between them lead to the lower parterre with a fountain and ornamental flower-beds. Around the parterre are open stands that include, amongst other things, large examples of the common (European) beech and its red-leafed

cultivar. The broad cross path with its low walls leading towards the Ball Court was known as the Central Platz (Summer Playground). In a central recess, facing the Royal Summer Palace, is the stone Hercules Fountain, named for its depiction of Hercules fighting the Hydra, a 1670 work by Jiří Bendl. The area is lined by rows of lime-trees and hornbeams.

To the right, the view of the Renaissance sgraffito facade of the remarkable Ball Court building on the edge of the Lower Stag Moat, originally designed by master builder Bonifác Wolmut in 1567–69, is striking. The statue of Night from the workshop of Matyáš Bernard Braun recalls the Baroque decoration of the garden before its bombardment in 1757. In the spring a band of rhododendrons flowers in front of the Ball Court. Massive pilasters divide the north facade of the Ball Court. The sgraffito decoration presents allegorical figures of the Sciences, Virtues and Elements. During renovations in 1952 a damaged section of the decoration was

19

replaced by an allegory of Industry with the symbol of the Five Year Plan. The building was actually used for ball games only for a short while. Already at the beginning of the 17th century its vault collapsed, and it was subsequently converted into a riding school and later stabling for horses. From the time of Joseph II to the beginning of the 20th century the building served the army; reconstruction began under Josip Plečnik after the foundation of Czechoslovakia. The Ball Court was the only architectural monument at Prague

⊿ *The northern facade of the Ball Court*
◀ *The eastern part of Orangery*

Chinese juniper ("kaizuka")
The Hercules Fountain by the Summer Ball Court / Scuplture of Night by M. B. Braun

The Fig House beneath the Royal Summer Palace

Castle to be destroyed during the Second World War – it burned to the ground during an assault on May 8ᵗʰ 1945, and had to be rebuilt from the foundations up. The vault and roofing were constructed in reinforced concrete to a design by Bedřich Hacar and the architect Pavel Janák completed the reconstruction in 1952. Since 1990 the

Ball Court has been used for cultural and social events.

The appearance of that part of the garden from the Ball Court towards the Royal Summer Palace is influenced by its arrangement in the English Landscape style. Among the various tree species here are the common (European) beech, Norway maple, sycamore, small-leaf linden, London plane, eastern (Canadian) hemlock, magnolia and common (English) yew. They are complemented by clumps of azaleas, rhododendrons, flowering maples, shrub peonies, roses and other plants. Three paths lead on from here – the central runs towards the Singing Fountain in front of the Royal Summer Palace (there were shady wicker arbours here previously), that on the left leads towards the garden wall on the Marian Ramparts, and that on the right follows the line of the Lower Stag Moat. The latter offers a view of the northern fortifications of the Castle with their defensive towers, overshadowed by St Vitus' Cathedral. Over time the view has been somewhat obscured by the trees growing in the Stag Moat. Coming right to the edge of the moat offers a view of the garden structures of the lower terrace, at the border between the Stag Moat and the Royal Garden. In the western part of the Orangery (also known previously as the Zwinger) stands an entirely new glasshouse, completed in 1999; designed by the architect Eva Jiřičná, it is equipped with modern technology governed automatically by computer. This original glasshouse replaces an earlier structure dating to the turn of the 1960's, and is designed for relaxation and private meetings on the part of the head of state, The Orangery continues down a grassy sward between two walls, stretching as far as beneath the garden around the Summer Palace.

Immediately beneath the Summer Palace another interesting structure can be seen – the massive perimeter wall of the Fig House (73 m x 12 m). This served for the cultivation of exotic, thermophilic

◄ *The Royal Summer Palace*
The upper parterre / The south slope of the Lower Stag Moat beneath the Summer Palace

The giardinetto *in the Royal Garden*
*Statue of Victory by J. Štursa in front of the Royal Summer Palace / The Singing
Fountain*

species from the very foundation of the Royal Garden until the First World War. It was erected by Maxmilian II at the beginning of the 1570's. The Fig House roof, made of planks and hay or straw is taken down every year in the spring and replaced in the autumn. The space is heated during the winter. In the summer the so-called "Italian dwarf trees" are moved to sunny spots within the garden. At the turn of the 1940's the Fig House underwent extensive structural repairs – windows were cut through to their original size and the damaged masonry secured. The tour continues towards the *giardinetto* in front of the Royal Summer Palace. In the Renaissance this took the form of a maze, formerly an inseparable part of all important gardens of the time. The famous Singing Fountain in the centre is a collaborative work of outstanding Italian and Czech Renaissance artists – it is made to a design by the painter Francesco Terzio and was modelled by Court Founder Tomáš Jaroš. The fountain was placed in 1573. The water, falls gradually into a broad lower basin where it chimes, so that directly beneath the basin, in particular, the fountain's song can be heard. The Royal Garden as a whole is closed at its eastern end by the famous Renaissance Royal (or Queen Anne's) Summer Palace. Its building was begun by Italian masters to a model by Paolo della Stella in 1538, and it was completed by the Court Master Builder Bonifác Wolmut in the 1560's. The Summer Palace's arcades are decorated with numerous figural reliefs with scenes from history and the philosophy of Antiquity. A relief with the figures of Ferdinand I and Queen Anne expresses the palace's dedication to the loving wife of the garden's founder, who died before her time.

This graceful garden building, designed for courtly entertainments, suffered war damage several times in the 17th and 18th centuries – indeed, from 1779 to 1838 the Royal Summer Palace was used by the army as an artillery laboratory. The balusters of the balustrade around the ground floor gallery were broken and replaced by a low wall. Once the army had left structural repairs were undertaken to designs by Pietro Nobile (in the 1840's). In the 20th century the Summer Palace was repeatedly repaired beginning in 1928–30, between 1952 and 1955 the building was stabilised, and maintenance

continues to this day. Balusters have again adorned the gallery since the 1980's. In 2001 visitors to Prague Castle had the for the first time the opportunity to glimpse the reconstructed, vaulted basement spaces, accessible from the Stag Moat, which once also served for the overwintering of thermophilic plants. Today the Summer Palace is mainly used for exhibitions.

History

Prior to the foundation of the Royal Garden, only the garden of the nuns of St George's Monastery is known from Prague Castle. There is no report at all of ornamental gardens in the immediate vicinity of the royal seat in the Middle Ages. The slopes of the Castle spur were extensively cultivated after the issuance of decrees for the founding of vineyards in Bohemia by the Emperor Charles IV in 1358. Plants to meet royal needs were supplied to the Court by various growers. Reports survive to show that later, several useful plants were grown in the Castle moat.

The Court garden on the high ground of Prague Castle was established after the ascent of the Habsburgs to the Czech royal

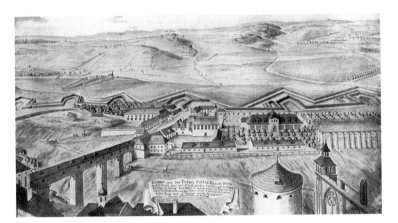

27

throne. Ferdinand I (1526–1564), after his election as King of Bohemia, intended to have his permanent seat at Prague Castle. At this time, and in connection with the new spiritual current, formal gardens were being established across Renaissance Europe at the courts of sovereigns, the nobility and ecclesiastical dignitaries. Ferdinand I and his successors were directly influenced by their sojourns in the royal courts of southern Europe, in particular in Spain. The narrow spur on which Prague Castle stands was not, however, suitable for the establishment of such gardens, and thus the

▲ *J. J. Dientzler: View of the principal tower of St Vitus' Cathedral across the Stag Moat from the north, pencil drawing, 1742*

◄ *F. Hogenberg: View of Prague Castle from the south and a panorama of Prague from Letna, copper engraving, c.1590*

area on the north side of the lower part of the Stag Moat, on thick loess beds, was selected. Beginning in the 1530's the area was obtained by the monarch through the gradual purchase from their owners of the vineyards then occupying it. In 1534 the northern

castle forefield was linked to the royal seat by a new bridge that later became known as the Powder Bridge *(Prašný most)*. The text has survived of a document concerning compensation for St George's Convent for leaving land to the monarch:

"We, Ferdinand, by Grace of God Roman, Hungarian, Bohemian, Dalmatian, Croatian etc. King etc... We hereby make known to all as aforetimes, when we began our new garden, that some part of the inheritance of St George's Monastery at Prague Castle we have decided to take and attach to our garden aforementioned. Desiring that the Abbess... of St George's Convent should not suffer from this, we desire

The Royal Summer Palace and part of the Royal Garden, copper engraving, 1666 (from Lucio Barreto's Historia Coelestis).

that for this usage ... every year a hogshead of our Svítnice wine from Prague should be set aside... ."
To establish his garden Ferdinand I summoned professionals who had obtained their experience in Italy, the Low Countries, Germany and other lands. On the land now surrounded by a new stone wall they sought those spots in which plants might be expected to grow particularly well. Despite many difficulties, within a few years the royal table was being graced by vegetables and fruit from the Royal Garden in Prague.

An important role in the creation of the garden was played by the emperor's second son, Archduke Ferdinand of the Tyrol. As the Royal Governor of Bohemia from 1547–1566, and in the absence of his father, he oversaw the work and made personal contributions to it. His involvement led to the discovery of new springs flowing from the Střešovice spur, and the bringing of water from thence to the castle along pipes; the water that had hitherto been drawn from the Brusnice stream and potable water from wells and springs was no longer sufficient to meet the Castle's needs. The creation of the Royal Garden was from the first accompanied by a shortage of money. Funds were raised from taxes, fines, loans and above all from Prague's Jewry. The Great Fire of 1541 which swept through the Lesser Quarter, Castle District and Castle itself had a huge negative impact on the first period of construction – the garden was damaged in several places and work was halted. Development of the garden continued under Maximilian II (1564–1576), even though as emperor he permanently shifted the Imperial seat from Prague to Vienna. Under Maximilian the aims of his father Ferdinand – who had expected the garden to be completed quickly with all due care – first reached their climax. It took several decades, however, before the garden attained its formal appearance with the completion of the Summer Palace and fountains. Many experts from lands in the west and south of Europe contributed to creating the Royal Garden. Among the architects and master builders these included in particular Paolo della Stella, Bonifác Wolmut and later Ulrico Aostallis, Giovani Gargiolli and Hans Vreedeman de Vries. The names of some of those who led the horticultural work are also known – the first Gardener, for example, was named Francesco and came from Vienna. Sound botanical advice was given to the Royal Court by the natural scientists Rembert Dodoens and Pietro Andrea Mattioli (d. 1577) – the latter also being personal physician to Emperor Ferdinand I, Archduke Ferdinand of the Tyrol and Emperor Maximilian. His herbal was published in Prague in an edition of Tadeáš Hájek of Hájek in 1562, and mentions the plants grown at Prague Castle. The garden was not only ornamental, but also practical. In addition to fruit trees and vines, vegetables, spices and curative plants were also grown here. Seedlings, bulbs, seeds and grafts were, according to surviving correspondence, ordered for example from cultivators in Trieste and Genoa. Thanks to the Emperor's Ambassador to the Turkish Sultan Aughier Ghislain de Busbecque, formerly tutor to Ferdinand I's children, plants hitherto unknown in Europe from the very distant lands of the East – such as the Turkish steppe and Syria – appeared in Prague: the Imperial Court began to be adorned by hyacinths, tulips, narcissuses, fritillaries etc. These exotic species, having acclimatised at Prague Castle, later spread further – in this way, for instance, tulips reached Holland. From the very beginning, the Emperor Ferdinand and his successors were interested in cultivating thermophilic plants such as orange, lemon, fig and pomegranate etc. In order to overwinter them a large stone building with a removable roof known as the Fig House was built below the Summer Palace, followed later by the nearby Orangery. Part of the garden was set aside for botanical curiosities obtained from distant lands. Various buildings designed for the entertainment of courtly society were gradually added to the garden, such as the Ball Court, Shooting Range, menageries and fish pools. Rudolf II (1576–1611), who selected Prague to be his seat, enlarged the northern castle bailey. He established the Pheasantry and built the pond. The Royal Garden was enlivened by courtiers and special guests. The Summer Palace was used not only for entertainment, but also for scientific study as an observatory by the Danish astronomer Tycho Brahe. Sports were played in the garden and in the ring close

31

to the east wall of the garden (now the Chotek Park). The solid Lion Court was erected for wild beasts. Contemporaries greatly admired the garden, and Rudolf spared no expense, while welcoming gifts to enrich it further. In subsequent years the Royal Garden, along with many other parts of the Castle, suffered not only from the removal of the Court from Prague, but in particular from the events of the Thirty Years' War. At the end of the 17th century the garden still retained its Renaissance character, but the first designs for its conversion into the Baroque were appearing. Under Leopold I (1657–1705) Baroque renovations were undertaken at the Castle that also affected the Royal Garden. From 1679–1680 the Emperor

Vincenc Morstadt: Hradčany from the east, 1830

and the Imperial Court found refuge from the Plague in Prague Castle, and the latter was thus enlivened once more by courtly entertainments. Close to the entrance to the Royal garden from the Powder Bridge the Lesser Ball Court was turned into a theatre. By

this time the 1670 fountain with the statue of Hercules by Jan Jiří Bendl already stood in the garden.

The conversion of the garden into the Baroque mode took place while the Royal Building Office was headed by Johann Heinrich Dienebier (1722–1748) and the Court Master Builder was the important architect Kilián Ignác Dientzenhofer (1730–1751). Gardeners from the Zinner family played an important part in the creation of the garden in the new style. According to surviving plans and engravings, the garden was a notable one with ornamental flower-beds on the upper parterre, and with a fountain and

Balustrade with putti and lions

sculptures complemented by symmetrical plantings on the lower parterre. The axis, running towards the middle of the Royal Summer Palace, was emphasised by overgrown pergolas. A considerable part of the garden was given over to practical use for grafting. The garden in front of the Summer Palace (the *giardinetto*) was also adapted to the Baroque. The expensively built new garden did not, however, have a long life, receiving no mercy in the wars of the reign of Maria Theresa (1740–1780). In 1757 Prussian artillery in positions west of Prague shelled Prague Castle and the Royal Garden, damaging the Baroque glasshouse (now part of the building of the former Presidential Residence), the Ball Court and the Summer Palace. The Theatre too was destroyed, along with one of a pair of statues from the workshop of Matyáš Bernard Braun, representing Day. In the second half of the 18ᵗʰ century the Empress Maria Theresa had the separate wings of Prague Castle rebuilt to designs by the Court Architect, a Viennese of Italian origin named Nicolo Paccassi. During these alterations the Powder Bridge was replaced by an earth causeway (1770). Various parts of the Castle, including the garden, began at this time to be used by the military.

During the 19ᵗʰ century the Royal Court visited Prague only rarely. Nevertheless, the castle gardens were gradually reworked in the Landscape style, the contributions of gardeners from the Weppl family (1772–1822) being particularly important in this regard. The transformation of the Royal Garden was completed by Court Gardener František Ritschl (1851–1882). The Baroque parterres were removed, and in place of the pergolas leading along the axis of the garden to the Summer Palace an avenue of plane trees was planted. The *giardinetto* by the Royal Summer Palace became a lawn. Trees and bushes were either raised especially or were brought from the Hvězda park and those around Imperial or noble stately homes. The military finally left the Royal Summer Palace, which they had occupied since the end of the 18ᵗʰ century, but the Ball Court served the army until as late as the beginning of the 20ᵗʰ century. A certain life returned to the Castle during the residence of the former Emperor Ferdinand V (1849–1875), a great lover of nature, and Empress Maria Anna (1849–1884), who loved walking in the garden.

After the establishment of the Czechoslovak Republic, President Masaryk, collaborating in particular with the architect Josip Plečnik, began to transform the neglected Castle in line with its ancient tradition into the modern seat of a head of state. Several projects for the restoration of the Royal Garden were also proposed, the majority of which came to nothing. A start was made with the renovation of the buildings in the garden – mainly the army-damaged Ball Court and Summer Palace. The gardeners of the Royal Garden devoted themselves primarily to the upkeep of the vegetation. The garden still retained its private character – it was opened to the general public only four times each year to mark holidays, and Alice Masaryková held occasional charity events here in support of the Red Cross. The reconstruction of the *giardinetto* in front of the Summer Palace (by Pavel Janák, Otakar Fierlinger, Jan Sokol) shortly before the Second World War was inspired by its Renaissance form. Work also began on renovating the trail beneath the Summer Palace, leading around the Renaissance Fig House and Orangery, at about the same time – to finish only recently, allowing its opening to the public at the beginning of the 2002 season. A careful restoration of the Singing Fountain was undertaken in 2001, and the Fig House was restored.

II. THE RIDING SCHOOL TERRACE GARDEN

Moving towards Prague Castle from the north along ul. U Prašného mostu, the Castle Riding School is on the right hand side. An attractive silhouette of the Castle buildings and the Cathedral Church of SS Vitus, Wenceslas & Adalbert (to give it its full name) is

easily available to those who take the inconspicuous entrance south of the main Riding School Entrance to reach the youngest of the Castle Gardens – the Riding School Terrace Garden. This was created in the 1950's on the roof of the garages then built, and was designed by the architect Pavel Janák using the morphological language of the Baroque gardens. It is open at regular hours throughout the year.

The Riding School Terrace Garden

THE RIDING SCHOOL TERRACE GARDEN

The street At the Powder

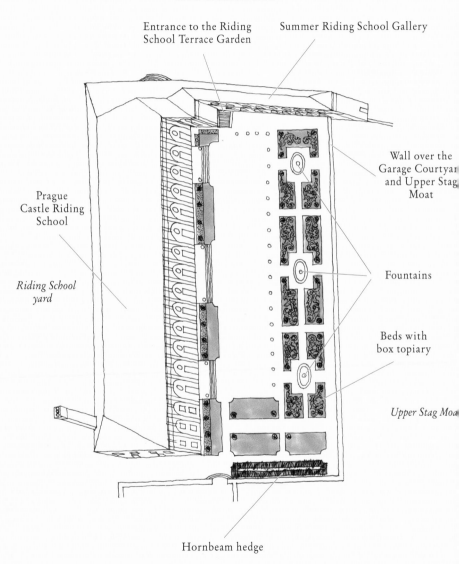

Entrance to the Riding
School Terrace Garden

Summer Riding School Gallery

Wall over the
Garage Courtyard
and Upper Stag
Moat

Prague
Castle Riding
School

*Riding School
yard*

Fountains

Beds with
box topiary

Upper Stag Moat

Hornbeam hedge

Pheasantry

Walk

Beyond the side entrance to the Riding School several steps lead to the terrace. To the north the garden is bounded by the Riding School itself, and to the east by the narrow, two-storey gallery. The Riding School and gallery were built to designs by the architect Jan Křtitel Mathey by the Castle Master Builder, Jan Antonín Canevale, in 1694. The cropped, double hedge of hornbeam on the west side hides the wall that separates the garden from the former Pheasantry. On the southern side, across the low wall on the edge of the Stag Moat, this roof garden offers a unique view of the northern defences of Prague Castle, and in particular of St Vitus' Cathedral – particularly atmospheric in the evening when seen by the lights installed on the northern side of the cathedral in 1995. The wooded Upper Stag Moat close to the terrace varies the view with the seasons. A considerable part of the garden area is strewn with light gravel, and white benches stand around its perimeter. Although the garden offers no shade, the three oval pools with their lightly flowing water in the middle of the beds with their ornamental topiary box trees and round yews bring refreshment to the parched terrace in the summer. Parterre lawns run parallel to the Riding School with autumn, spring and summer plantings. Plečnik's vases of spring--flowering annuals are an attractive complement to the rest of the roof garden.

History

The site on which the garden was to be established was known historically as the Summer Riding School. This originated, along with the covered Riding School, at the end of the 17th century, and as its name suggests horses were exercised and equestrian games took place here. The long gallery on the east side was for spectators. This space was also used for the extraordinary theatrical event held to mark the coronation of Charles VI in 1723 – the world premiere of the Italian opera *Constanza e Fortezza* ('Constancy and Fortitude') by the Viennese Court Composer Jan Josef Fux. A wooden amphitheatre for an audience of several thousand was built specifically for the occasion to a design by the Imperial Architect Giuseppe Galli-Bibiena. The night-time performance was lit by several thousand wax candles and hanging lamps.

The history of the Riding School and its environs from the end of the 18th century onwards was less illustrious – the building and areas around it were used for military purposes. In later decades this was the working courtyard of Prague Castle. A century ago, E. Tonner wrote: *"...After the residence of Ferdinand the Gracious in Prague this former riding school was used for storing summer fuel, and this was such a large stockpile that it could have made several even in the not underserved folds of Podskalí (the Rafters' Quarter)...".* Before the Second World War the area of the Summer Riding School was occupied by a tennis court. From 1946 reconstruction of the Riding School to serve for exhibitions was undertaken to designs by Castle Architect Pavel Janák. After 1948 it was decided to build garages on the site of the former Summer Riding School.Skeletal remains discovered during earth-moving works in 1951 were later shown to relate to an extensive Early Medieval cemetery in the northern bailey. Janák included a proposal for establishing a garden in the immediate vicinity in his designs for reconstructing the Riding School; the conversion of the terrace into a garden was finished in 1957 by the architect Vladimír Tintěr. Subsequently the garden was one of the few in the Castle freely open to the public. The garden is currently used for cultural events. International festivals of ethnic music have been held here, and young artists too have been inspired by its atmosphere: Tomáš Kotík – a young artist living in the USA who is the great-great-grandson of the first Czechoslovak president, T. G. Masaryk – experimentally installed his metal objects here.

St Vitus' Cathedral from the Riding School Terrace Garden

THE BASTION GARDEN

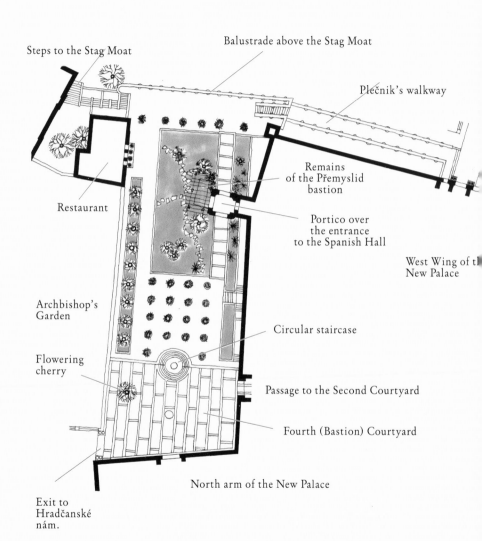

Steps to the Stag Moat

Balustrade above the Stag Moat

Plečnik's walkway

Restaurant

Remains
of the Přemyslid
bastion

Portico over
the entrance
to the Spanish Hall

West Wing of the
New Palace

Archbishop's
Garden

Circular staircase

Flowering
cherry

Passage to the Second Courtyard

Fourth (Bastion) Courtyard

North arm of the New Palace

Exit to
Hradčanské
nám.

III. THE BASTION GARDEN

Somewhat to the side of the most frequently visited parts of Prague Castle, above the Stag Moat and immediately adjacent to the Archbishop's Garden (from which it is separated by a high wall), is the Bastion Garden, the name of which recalls the medieval fortifications. This garden is open at regular hours all year.

Walk

The Bastion Garden in the north-west corner of the Castle can be reached from the Powder Bridge via Plečnik's walkway over the Stag Moat beneath the windows of the Spanish Hall, through a passage from the Castle's Second Courtyard or even directly from Hradčanské nám. The Fourth (Bastion) Courtyard is paved with cobbles in geometric patterns, beneath which fragments of a Romanesque house were found. The Romanesque Church of the Virgin, discovered nearby, is believed to have been the earliest Christian sanctuary anywhere in Prague Castle – its foundations can be seen behind glass in the passage to the Second Courtyard. In the western corner of the courtyard a dark pink Japanese flowering cherry blooms in the spring. An original circular staircase bridges the difference in height between the Fourth Courtyard and the terrace that is home to the actual garden. On both sides of the staircase the edge of the terrace is lined by replicas of Plečnik's vases set with Dracaenas. Another regular line is formed by the ornamental acacias along the wall of the neighbouring garden of the Archbishop's Palace, while on the north side are six, somewhat older topiary Thujas. The southern part of the garden is covered in white marble gravel and articulated by eighteen regularly-spaced Thujas. This geometric section adjoins a grassy space with irregularly-spaced, inset stones, and freely positioned trees – reminiscent overall of a Japanese garden. Hybrid white firs grow here, along with

a pagoda tree graft and a pyramidal oak. Beneath a pergola draped with wisteria, trumpet creeper and ivy, by the Theresean portico leading to the Spanish Hall, lie the hidden remains of a bastion dating to the time of Přemysl Otakar II (the "Iron and Golden King"). In the north-western corner of the garden, overlooking the

*The portico over the entrance to the Spanish Hall / The balustrade above the Stag Moat
Detail of the circular staircase / Flowering cherry in the Fourth (Bastion) Courtyard*

Stag Moat, stands a garden restaurant built in the 1950's, originally as a pavilion with an open terrace. The garden ends with a white gravel path in front of a granite balustrade over the Stag Moat. Plečnik underpinned the terrace with a free arcade on the site where the castle embankment comes to an end. After the Second World War the arches were blocked up and a shelter was thus created for

President Emil Hácha. From here it is possible to descend by a stairway of coarse, undressed stones into the Stag Moat, or come by an oblique stair on the other side and Plečnik's walkway on a free-standing arcade to the Powder Bridge.

History

At the zenith of the Middle Ages this area lay between two moats and defensive walls with towers. After the ascent of the Habsburgs to the Bohemian throne Prague Castle underwent extensive alterations – at this time the second moat was filled in and an armoury was built above the Hradčany ravine. Equally, renovations under Maria Theresa left their mark on this part of the Castle, too – a new castle wing bounded the Bastion Courtyard to the east and south, the bastion was liquidated, the old armoury building was demolished, the Hradčany ravine was filled in, and the wooden bridge which had previously led into the castle from the west removed. Interest in this part of the Castle was revived in the 1860's and 1870's for practical reasons associated with the planned, but never realised, coronation of Francis Joseph I. It was necessary to arrange an entrance into the Spanish Hall. A cross-wall divided the courtyard into two parts, and was pierced symmetrically in two places by decorative screen gates. A path led from the gates to the portico leading into the Spanish Hall, and on the other side gave out into the fore part of the courtyard through a second set of gates; this bordered a lawn in which trees later grew freely. Above the Stag Moat was a wall containing loopholes. A decorative screen closed the Bastion Courtyard in the direction of Hradčanské nám. This part of the Castle spur was newly and completely renovated after the creation of Czechoslovakia. Once again, the plans – realised in 1932 – were by Castle Architect Josip Plečnik, who had been given the task of reconstructing the somewhat derelict Bastion Courtyard with a garden. A notable garden of timeless form, evoking memories of

the Mediterranean, came into being; the arrangement respected the earlier division of the spaces now known as the Fourth Courtyard and the Bastion Garden.

Trampled stones in the grass and the pergola over the remains of the Přemyslid bastion

THE SOUTH GARDENS

The Paradise, Rampart and Hartig Gardens are three mutually related wholes, running the entire length of the Castle's southern facade. They arose gradually on the site of former fortifications. The Hartig Garden was originally a palace garden, belonging to the Hartig Palace in the Lesser Quarter. The rampart linking the southern facade to Hradčanské nám. and set with an avenue was designed as early as the mid–18th century by the Viennese architect Nicolo Paccassi; the concept was only realised, however, under President T. G. Masaryk in the 1920's by the architect Josip Plečnik. The latter was able to use the distinctive character of this site, protected to the north by the Castle palace buildings and facing the sun. The unique views of the stone city with its green islands, overshadowed by churches, towers and turrets, invites pause. The restrained and harmonious composition of spaces, lawns, trees and shrubs with architectural elements in no way detracts from them. The South Gardens can be reached either from Hradčanské nám. to the west, with an entrance immediately next to the Castle Steps, from the East Gate on ul. Na Opyši, from the Third Court via the staircase in the New Palace building or even from the south, through the palace gardens of the Lesser Quarter (the Ledeburg, Lesser and Greater Pálffy, Kolowrat and Lesser Fürstenberg gardens). The gardens were opened to the public at weekends only from 1960, and then at regular opening times throughout the Summer season from 1993.

► *Royal Paulownia in the Rampart Garden*

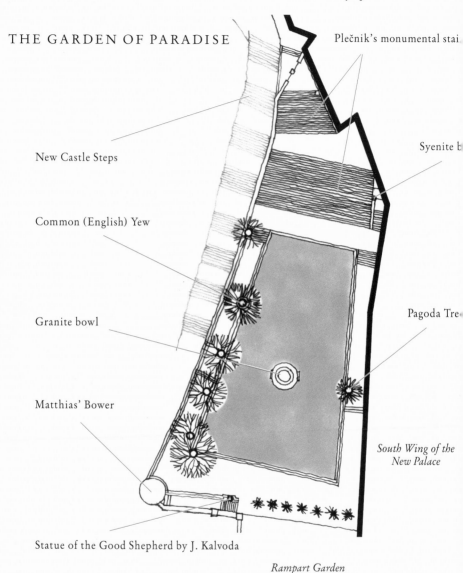

The Hradčany Square

THE GARDEN OF PARADISE

Plečnik's monumental stai

New Castle Steps

Syenite b

Common (English) Yew

Granite bowl

Pagoda Tre

Matthias' Bower

South Wing of the
New Palace

Statue of the Good Shepherd by J. Kalvoda

Rampart Garden

IV. THE GARDEN OF PARADISE

Walk

A discreet entrance next to the Castle Steps gives onto the monumental stair of the Garden of Paradise. The latter is bounded to the south by ramparts dating to 1849 while to the north it its closed

by the wall of the South Wing of the New Palace (which attained is present appearance in renovations undertaken in the time of Maria Theresa). The garden entrance is decorated with a sandstone amphora, and on the stair is a flat bowl of black syenite. Plečnik's original design for the placing of a monolith – a monument to the Legionnaires – next to the entrance was not realised, and only its

Granite bowl in the Garden of Paradise

foundation remained underground. Masaryk, however, did not forget the idea, and the monolith later became part of the Third Court within the Castle. The interesting space beneath the staircase is used for occasional exhibitions. The greater part of the Garden of Paradise comprises a grassy parterre with a great bowl made of Mrákotín granite in the centre. The garden offers an opportunity to see the oldest tree at Prague Castle – a common (English) yew estimated to be some 400 years old. The extension of the garden wall above the Castle Steps ends in an elegant, Renaissance structure known as Matthias' Bower (as it dates to 1617, i.e. to the reign of the Emperor Matthias, brother of Rudolf II). Every day, assuming that the outside temperature is above −5°C, a fanfare rings out from here to mark the tenth hour. The walls of the pavilion are decorated with paintings by the renowned Czech artist Josef Navrátil (1798–1865), while on the ceiling are painted arms dating to the 17th century. Of Navrátil's numerous paintings decorating the interior of Prague Castle, these are the only ones to survive. The Garden of Paradise ends with the remains of a Baroque wall behind the Bower. Past the 1922 sculpture of the Good Shepherd by J. Kalvoda and beyond the row of pyramidal hornbeams the Rampart Garden begins.

History

A garden was originally founded here on a filled-in moat by Archduke Ferdinand of the Tyrol in the mid-16th century at his newly-erected Renaissance seat – the New Building, which later became part of the South Wing of the New Palace. It was used by the Emperor Rudolf II as an intimate palace garden on the sunny, southern side of the Castle. Rare plants grew here, a belvedere and an aviary were included, and the emperor also had his spa here. By the end of the 17th century the garden had been let go, and the Court Gardener was therefore ordered to restore it. For this reason it was divided into two terraces – fruit trees, vines and ornamental shrubs were grown here, while tulips or "blue lilies" were also introduced. In the first half of the 18th century the Archduke Ferdinand's old

◄ *The Garden of Paradise*
Part of the southern facade of the Castle overgrown with creepers
Statue of the Good Shepherd by J. Kalvoda, 1922

belvedere was removed and the garden transformed in the Baroque style. During the 19th century the garden gradually changed to reflect the Landscape style, but by the beginning of the 20th century was uncared for. An architectural contest was arranged to resolve this situation, for which primarily Romantic proposals were submitted. President Masaryk ultimately selected the simple but

52

monumental project suggested by the architect Josip Plečnik – who as Castle Architect would later also create the adjacent Rampart Garden and carry out a range of other projects at the Castle.

Matthias' Bower in the Garden of Paradise

V. THE RAMPART GARDEN

Walk

In summer, the water from the 1703 Baroque fountain moved here from the Garden of Paradise pleasantly refreshes the air. The neighbouring lawns are lined by trimmed yew hedges. Among the trees to be found either in the lawns or directly on the footpaths are japonica, dawn redwood, weeping copper beech and a rare Royal Paulownia (Empress or Princess Tree), the largest example in this country – it's bluish bell-flowers appear in the spring before its new shoots. The garden paths lead to a semi-circular look-out offering a view of the Lesser Quarter, dominated by the dome of St Nicholas' Church. Beneath the look-out it is possible to reach the Hartig Garden on the southern Terrace. Opposite the look-out, within the front of the Castle Palace building, are the original steps – known as the Bull Stair – leading up to the Third Courtyard. Beneath the stairs grows a rare 'evergreen' Turner's oak' *(Quercus pseudoturneri)*. Continuing onwards, the mass of the Prague Castle buildings too gradually changes on the left-hand side. The Ludwig Wing protrudes from the Old Royal Palace, known to history as the site of the infamous 1618 Defenestration when bureaucrats of the Governor's Office were thrown from the first floor onto the rampart – where their lives were saved by the sloping terrain and mass of rubbish. This event, which foreshadowed the Thirty Years' War, is recalled by two 17th century memorials to Vilém Slavata of Chlum and Jaroslav Bořita of Martinice. The composition of the garden is shaped at several points by architectural details dating to Plečnik's renovations in the 1920's and by historic sculptures newly installed here. A golden marlstone pyramid close to the look-out is the most conspicuous landmark. The female bust above the gate to the Alpinum is by the sculptor D. Pešan, a contemporary of Plečnik's. Not far from the Bellevue look-out pavilion are original 18th century sculptures of torchbearers by Ignác Platzer. Opposite stands a 1920's fountain decorated with the arms of Slovakia and a Baroque Hercules. Other works of art are also to be found here. Among the trees are an Indian Bean tree *(Catalpa bignoioides)* from the Mississippi Valley, with large, heart-shaped leaves, in July bearing white bell-flowers with purple dapples. Its fruits - seed pods up to 40 cm long – remain on the tree until spring. Close to the gardener's shed grows an interesting Kentucky coffee tree *(Gymnokladus dioicus)* with obvious, up to 80 cm long, pinnate leaves, white flowers in composite panicles, and seeds in pods up to 20cm long. It buds only when other trees already have their full foliage. The weeping beech *(Fagus sylvatica Pendula)* is bizarre in its growth habit, with strong branches reaching almost to the ground. The uniqueness of the garden rests in its inimitable views over Prague, made possible by the lowering of the walls in the mid–19th century. Look-outs appeared at several points along the Rampart Garden to designs by Plečnik – that with mosaic tiling (the Little Look-out above the Hartig Garden) is particularly charming. The largest pavilion is the Bellevue on the terrace beneath the wall of the Foundation for Noble Ladies, with its monumental columnar architecture. Furthest to the east stands the Moravian Bastion with a striking granite obelisk topped by an Ionian capital (the so-called "stela"); President Masaryk would take his ease at the stone table here. It is from here, too, that the Castle vineyards can be seen, planted with the resistant Hybernal strain, and with shrubs grown in the form of an upright cordon, connected to the Alpinum, again currently undergoing restoration. On one of the terraces below the principal path a memorial linden shoot – the Millennium Tree – was planted on October 28th, 2000. Since 1995, and after their rehabilitation, the palace gardens of the Lesser Quarter have gradually been opened to the

---

▶ *The Bellevue Pavilion*
The Alpinum on the south slope of the Rampart Garden

Fountain with a statue of Hercules / The Little Look-out
Granite obelisk by the Moravian Bastion / Pyramid next to the look-out in the
Rampart Garden

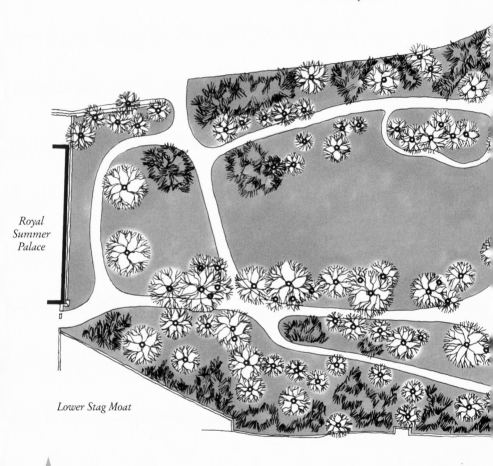

Marian Ramparts

*Royal
Summer
Palace*

Lower Stag Moat

0   10   20   30   40 m

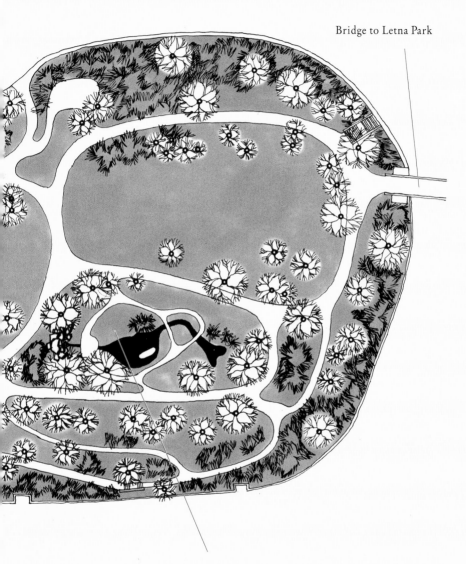

Bridge to Letna Park

Julius Zeyer Memorial and pool

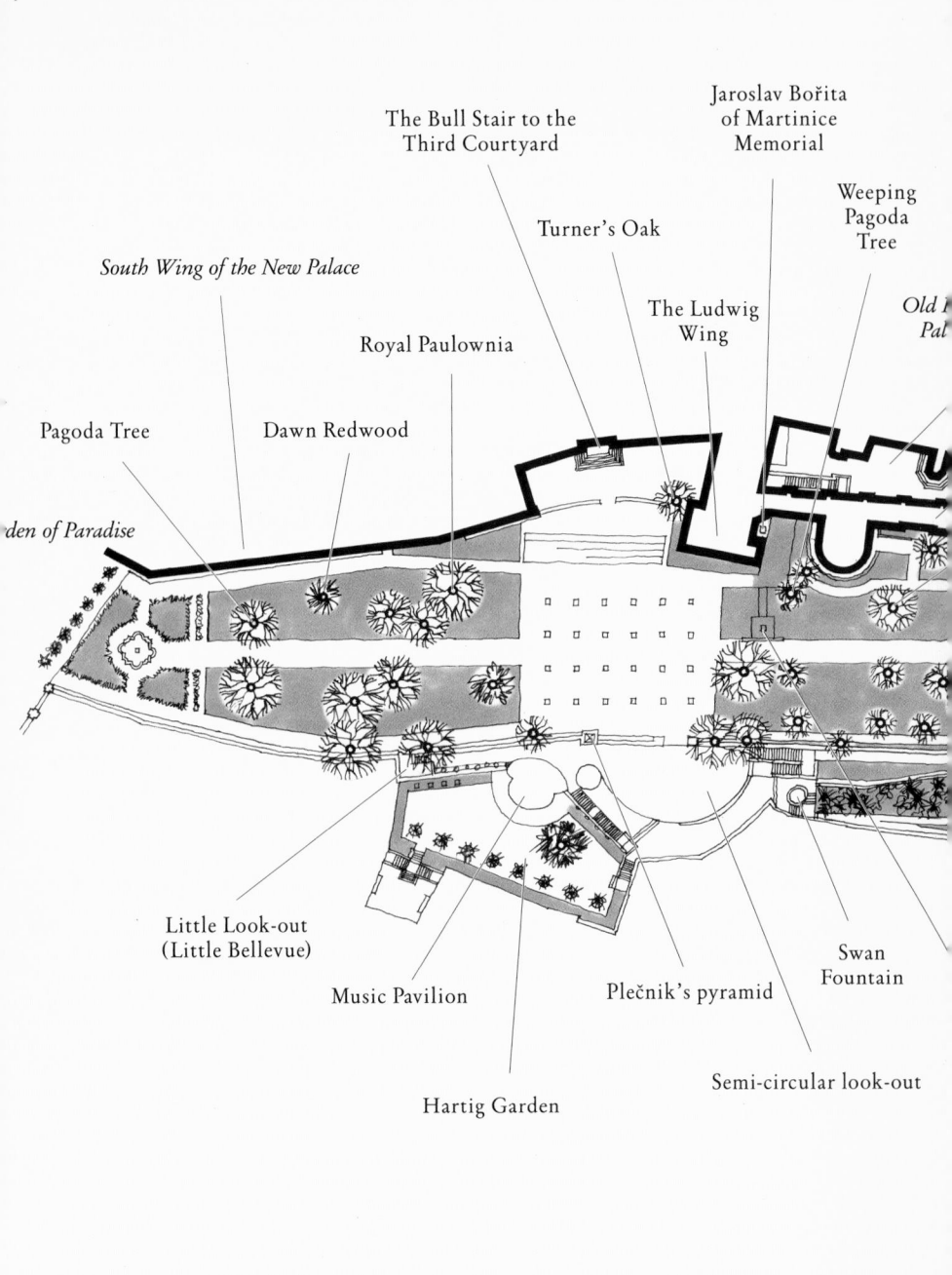

The Bull Stair to the
Third Courtyard

Jaroslav Bořita
of Martinice
Memorial

Turner's Oak

Weeping
Pagoda
Tree

South Wing of the New Palace

Royal Paulownia

The Ludwig
Wing

*Old P
Pal*

Pagoda Tree

Dawn Redwood

den of Paradise

Little Look-out
(Little Bellevue)

Music Pavilion

Plečnik's pyramid

Swan
Fountain

Semi-circular look-out

Hartig Garden

public on the south slopes beneath Prague Castle, most now cared for by the State Institute for Heritage Care. For visitors, the linkage of the palace and the castle gardens is convenient, as in the peak season it is possible to walk down from Prague Castle directly to Valdštejnské nám. in the Lesser Quarter and *vice versa*. The project for the rehabilitation of the palace gardens on the southern slopes beneath the Castle has been supported by the Prague Heritage Fund, founded by Charles, Prince of Wales. The walk through the South Gardens, some 400 m long in all, ends by the Lobkowicz Palace, where the Rampart Garden narrows and gives out through a gate on the easternmost part of the Castle spur – Opyš – from which it possible to descend via the Old Castle Steps to Klárov and the Malostranská Metro station and tram stop.

History

The rampart on the southern side of Prague Castle was overgrown with grass and thickets. It was for this reason that the fire which broke out on June 2nd 1541 in the Lesser Quarter spread so quickly here, and was fed by the wooden buildings in Hradčany beneath the southern Castle outwork. Various Castle staff lived in the many small penthouses here. Gardens belonging to Castle's staff began to appear along the southern wall of the palace, built entirely during the reign of Maria Theresa, at the end of the 18th century. Among those to have a garden here, for example, were the Castle Inspector and doctor Josef Rudolph (fl. 1780–1816) and his successors. There were further gardens along the wall of the Theresean Foundation for Noble Ladies and beyond, beneath the southern windows of the Lobkowicz Palace. In 1849 the whole rampart was enclosed within a new wall. Preparations for the (ultimately cancelled) coronation of Francis Joseph I as King of Bohemia in the second half of the 19th century were the impetus for a redesign of the Garden of Paradise and the rampart. The Viennese Court decided that the author of the

new proposals, in the Landscape style, was to be Court Gardener František Ritschl. The park finished in 1863 was gradually neglected in later years.

An entirely newly conceived monumental work founded in a simple

artistic design and with a range of artistic elements resulted from the extensive reconstruction of the South Gardens undertaken in 1921–24 to designs by Josip Plečnik, and is a tribute to the creativity of this Slovene architect, supported by President Masaryk. These two strong personalities mutually influenced and respected one another, and between them there arose a relationship comparable to the relationship between Humanist-oriented patrons and artists /architects in the Renaissance. Plečnik was inspired by the architecture of the Mediterranean but at the same time respected the local historical structural elements, and his solutions also incorporated rare plants, such as the old yew that is the curiosity of

The Vilém Slavata Memorial / The Ludwig Wing

the Garden of Paradise. In place of the old, semi–circular bastion he proposed a glasshouse, the upper part of which served as a terrace with a view over Prague. In the 1960's this was torn down, and the present terrace and a new staircase were designed by the architects

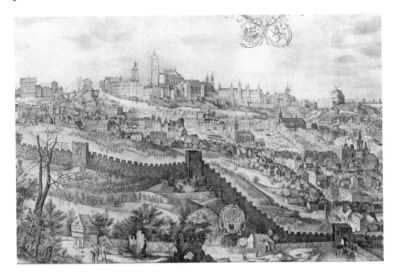

59

Podzemný and Beneš. In the space occupied by the rest of the Přemyslid bastion Plečnik placed a voliére – but even this is no longer extant. Demanding structural work was required to fix the southern slope beneath the Rampart Garden in 1926–1927; the terraces created were used to establish an alpinum and vineyard. The South Gardens underwent extensive reconstruction in 1987–1993, and their formal opening was accompanied by the publication of a book entitled *Zahrady Pražského hradu* ('The Gardens of Prague Castle').

Joh. Wechter after Filip van der Bossche: Prague, 1606, copper engraving

VI. THE HARTIG GARDEN

This garden can be reached down steps from the look-out in the Rampart Garden, and attained its current appearance in alterations carried out in the 1960's. It comprises two small terraces set beneath

high buttressing walls. The propitious, sheltered location with its warm microclimate is reflected in the rambling plants such as Parthenocissi and thermophilic wisteria. There is ivy here, too, despite its usual preference for shady locations. In the middle of the upper terrace there are fragrant rose bushes. The garden also contains Baroque statues of the gods of Antiquity, brought here from the château park at Štiřín – these come from the workshop of

▲ *The steps to the Hartig Garden*
► *The Music Pavilion in the Hartig Garden*
   Statues from the workshop of M. B. Braun

the sculptor Matyáš Bernard Braun, where they were fashioned by his nephew Antonín in the 1730's. In the summer months visitors may listen to early evening concerts or see theatrical performances in the intimate atmosphere of the garden. The garden was founded sometime after 1670 by Isabela Švihovská née ze Salmu by the newly-built palace. Around 1720 the palace was rebuilt by its new owner, Count Josef Hartig, who also had a Baroque music pavilion erected in the garden. In the 1960's the Hartig Garden passed into the hands of Prague Castle.

VII. ST WENCESLAS' VINEYARD

Leaving the South Gardens by Castle's Eastern Gate at Opyš and descending the Old Castle Steps, the high wall on the left hides St Wenceslas' Vineyard from view. On the north side it virtually abuts the Chotek road. At the present time it is not open to the public.

History

The vineyard takes its name from a legend associated with St Wenceslas, who supposedly "begged of his father a plot where a vineyard could be planted, that the wine made might serve the needs of Mass. And when such a site he was granted close to the Castle, at once he created his vineyard, rearing vines, the wine from the grapes of which he himself pressed and prepared for the churches". According to surviving written records, however, the vineyard was founded by Charles IV in 1375, and at that time was called Opyš. The designation 'St Wenceslas' Vineyard' first appears in the second half of the 17th century. St Wenceslas' Vineyard is shown on a Prague vista as early as 1562. Several buildings lay within the vineyard grounds; according to an assessment of the vineyard which preceded its sale at the end of the 18th century, these were a house with a shingle roof next to the Old Castle Steps, with a cellar cut into the rock, a winery house with a shingle roof comprising three rooms and finally a wine press of medium size.

Over the centuries various owners held title to the vineyard itself, among whom were prominent figures from the ecclesiastical and secular worlds, noblemen, craftsmen and bureaucrats including the chaplain Petr of Říčany, the tailor Wenceslas, one Matěj Konstantin, the book printer and burgher of the Lesser Borough of Prague Bartoloměj Netolický, David Florýn of Lambštejn, the Castle building scribe from the time of Rudolf II, the Imperial Counsellor

63

Pavel Michna of Vacínov, Lord of Konopiště & Tloskov, and the Imperial Chamberlain and General Don Wilhelm Verdugo – the vineyard thus became known as the Verdugo Vineyard, and from the second half of the 17th century was managed as such by the Šliks. The vineyard passed into the hands of the Metropolitan Chapter of St

Vitus in 1751 as a legacy from Prince Štěpán Kinský, in consequence of erroneous notions to which he had at some time adhered. In 1799 the Chapter sold the vineyard to the Imperial & Royal Courier of the Supreme Postal Office, Tomáš František Richter, whose family would retain it for almost a century and a half. In the 1830's the owners built themselves a villa here, and a glasshouse was built later. At this time radical changes were made to the area around the rocky Opyš spur and the new line of communication now known as the Chotek road was opened up, as part of which the northern slopes of

Path in St Wenceslas' Vineyard

the vineyard plot were also altered. During the 19th century the vines cultivated in St Wenceslas' Vineyard gradually gave way to fruit and ornamental trees.

After the Second World War the land of the former St Wenceslas' Vineyard and the buildings thereon were confiscated from the members of the Richter family as German citizens. After a transitional period of nationalised administration lasting until 1956 these properties passed into the ownership of the Czechoslovak state, and were used by the Diplomatic Service and later the Ministry of Interior. In the 1960's a project was proposed for the reconstruction of St Wenceslas' Vineyard with a sketch of the then state of its vegetation – only six aged vines were to be found. The proposal called for the establishment of "a smaller vineyard to recall the ancient one on the site", the establishment of which would use the middle part of the southern slope, where in thin (2 x 2 m) clumps it should have been possible to plant some 225 vines in circles and perhaps 15 in lines on the terrace pergolas. The St Wenceslas' Vineyard area was taken under the care of the Office of the President of the Republic in 1990. Within the framework for new renovations to Prague Castle and in an attempt to make it as accessible as possible to the public, a new project was commissioned for the restoration of the area. In addition to the reconstruction of the villa itself, the terraces and the paths giving access thereto, this assumed an overall revitalisation of the garden, including the renewal of the vineyard proper. Cuttings of various musty European strains, both white and blue, were planted on the lower southern slope and over supporting structures. The production of microsamples of actual wine is also presumed. The longitudinal divide of the south slope consists of a footpath and supporting wall that will again be decorated with a vine-draped pergola.

The upper half of the slope will have the character of a flowery meadow, with primarily thermophilic and steppe perennials, including curative and aromatic plants. The shrubbery will be kept

65

to modest dimensions. The upper edge and the steep northern slope remain covered by trees, and a certain replenishment of the trees is presumed. St Wenceslas' Vineyard offers unusual views over the historic centre of Prague.

View towards Klárov from St Wenceslas' Vineyard

VIII. THE PHEASANTRY

West of the Castle Riding School between the Stag Moat and ul. Mariánské hradby lies the green area of the former Pheasantry. Today this area is part of the Castle's horticultural gardens, and is not open to the public. Fruit trees in particular are grown here, along with various ornamental shrubs and flowers for the decoration of the formal spaces within Prague Castle.

History   67

The land here became sovereign property in 1594, during the reign of Rudolf II – the date has remained clear to this day above the western gate through the surviving part of the Renaissance walls close to the garden office. According to a 1732 note by the scribe Dienebier a breeder's house stood within the Pheasantry, along with several working buildings – a grain store and two pheasant chambers, immediately adjacent to these two wire pheasant runs. In the eastern part of the Pheasantry Emperor Rudolf II had a fish pond established "by our will and for our pleasure", as shown by written sources. This was filled with utility water from the series of pools at Litovice and Hostivice, and from here water was also distributed to other parts of the Castle. The pond was stocked with fish and various water fowl nested here, including ducks, swans and "laughing birds". Ice from the pond was used during the year for chilling food in the Castle cellars. Even now the pond and its surroundings are an oasis of calm, the noise from Jelení ul. over the wall not penetrating. The western part of the Pheasantry was used for the actual rearing of pheasants and partridges brought here not only from the Imperial estates but also from abroad (the Netherlands). Oversight of the Pheasantry was entrusted to the pheasant keepers who, while under the Royal Building Office answered professionally to the Master of the Hunt. The

responsibility of the office was to provided plumed game to the Imperial table thrice yearly in appropriate quantities. The income of the Pheasantry keepers in the 17th century also came from their right to have beer and wine on tap, and to the yields of fruit and grass. The Pheasantry suffered considerable damage during the Thirty Years'

War, particularly during the occupation of the Swedes in 1648–49. From official documents it is possible to assess how the situation appeared after the departure of the Swedish soldiery – the rear building used for breeding pheasants was completely ruined, and demolished, while the Swedes' use of the Pheasantry to bury their dead from an outbreak of plague meant that artisans were unwilling to enter there. These graves were later filled with lime.

The Pheasantry suffered further damage at the hands of French

The Rudolphine pond in the eastern part of the Pheasantry

forces at the beginning of the 1740's. After the results of the French assault had been cleared away the court poultry farm was established in the pheasant chambers and the perimeter walls and gates restored. In 1750 a contract was agreed with Imperial Engineer Major K. Cremeri for the lease of part of the Pheasantry to be used to raise mulberries, whereby the lessee also had the right to draw beer and take advantage of other perks. In 1757 Prussian artillery returned the Pheasantry to ruins – "fireballs" and bombs damaged the working buildings and poultry runs, and the mulberry plantation too was destroyed. In 1795 another pond was established to serve as a reservoir in case of fire, but also as a place for taking horses into water (this being filled in in the 1980's). The Pheasantry was subsequently rented out to Castle staff, and from the second half of the 19th century until 1918 it was used by the Château Hetman. From 1971–77 archaeological excavations were undertaken across an extensive area west of the Riding School, during which a rich cemetery was revealed which probably contained the remains of members of the princely retinue of the late 9th to early 11th centuries. The continuation of the Early Medieval cemetery was revealed on the site of the Riding School and adjacent terrace.

69

IX. THE LUMBE GARDEN

The area known as the Lumbe Garden is adjacent to the Pheasantry and originally stretched from the latter as far as the northern and western Hradčany walls. To the south it is closed by the Nový Svět moat – a continuation of the Stag Moat interrupted by ul. U Brusnice. The Office of the President of the Republic purchased this land in 1925 from the heirs of surgeon Karel Lumbe, who had come into possession of it in the 1860's. The largest part of the garden comprises a field and garden formerly belonging to the Černín family, who occupied an extensive palace not far away in Hradčany. In the second half of the 19th century Lumbe began to divide the land into building plots, but only a small part of his plan was carried out. In 1911 the U Brusnice road for an electric railway was built across the Lumbe Garden to Pohořelec, and further separation of plots was halted. During the 20th century architectural proposals for using the area were repeatedly drawn up, until a competition for its alteration was announced and judged in 1995. From the 1920's onwards the area served as a supply garden to the Office of the President of the Republic, as it now does for the Prague Castle Administration. The fruit trees here yield excellent fruit, and the market gardens here with all their glasshouses, hothouses, flowerbeds and racks have always served for the cultivation of the cut flowers, pot plants and decorative leaves needed to decorate the interiors and courtyards of Prague Castle. They manage to supply the Castle's entire demand for a wide assortment of fresh flowers at all times except during the greatest state visits. It is here, too, that all of the material needed to create ornamental beds, outdoor flower arrangements and balcony planters is grown. In the past, the garden also supplied virtually all of the home-grown vegetables to the President's kitchen.

X . THE STAG MOAT

In the Middle Ages Prague Castle was defended to the north not only by ramparts but also by the natural ravine of the Brusnice stream. The last great rampart building above the Stag Moat was undertaken in the 15th century during the reign of Wladislaw Jagiello. At the present time both parts of the Stag Moat, newly linked by a pedestrian tunnel, are open to the public. The Moat can be reached either from the newly-built path from Klárov or from the Powder Bridge, from which both halves are accessible.

71

Walk

The Stag Moat can truly be called unique – in the centre of the metropolis, in close proximity to the seat of the Head of State, it is an untamed natural environment in which birds and small animals live. The Upper Stag Moat was opened to the public during the period of the First Republic, when the bears given to President T. G. Masaryk by Legionnaires returning from Siberia and Transcarpathia (Ruthenia) lived here – indeed, the last bear still lived here at the beginning of the 1960's. In 1996 the Moat was again opened to the public to mark the end of an extensive exhibition devoted to Castle Architect J. Plečnik.

From the Powder Bridge it is possible to see the route that leads to the path running to the north slope and on to a small vineyard – the

Plečnik's Vineyard

Masaryk's Look-out

latter proposed by Plečnik in the 1920's and recalling the original use of the moat's sides. At the present time sixty grapevines of various strains grow here: in addition to the noble Rhenish Riesling – known as the wine of kings and king of wines – these include recent hybrids of American and European vines. Here, however, they are decorative in character, even if in good years they are able to provide visitors with refreshment in the form of mature bunches of grapes during autumn walks to Masaryk's look-out. Around the old small-leafed limes *(Tilia cordata)* Plečnik built a semi-circular look-out that was a favourite of Masaryk's, from which there is an interesting panorama of the houses in Hradčany and the peak of Petřín hill and its tower. In this quiet, refined space above the crowns of the trees visitors can devote themselves to uninterrupted meditation or lovers' trysts... The look-out and winegrove, which had long lain in ruins, were restored in the 1990's. A few dozen metres away to the rear, along the axis of the look-out, Plečnik's apiary stands among the trees in the orchard. The valley floor can be reached down an oblique path cut into the slope. The pleasant microclimate and the Brusnice stream give rise here to a mix of native and domesticated trees, such as maples, ashes, chestnuts, hornbeams, larches, yews, limes, acacias etc. Tennis courts stand at the western end of the Moat. The path along the valley floor leads to the 1950's cottage for the bear warden, next to which there was formerly a bear pit. The sandstone statue of the Night-watchman by F. Úprka was given to President Masaryk by former students from Hořice. The Lower Stag Moat was never open to the public in the 20th century, even though its use for walks is known from the end of the 19th century. In 1999 the path leading from Klárov to the Lower Stag Moat was created, giving out at the Powder Bridge. From a depth of 30 m it is possible to wonder at the architecture of the Castle's northern fortifications – Dalibor's Tower (the Daliborka),

72

▶ *The Lower Stag Moat*

The Masaryk Look-out in the Upper Stag Moat
Plečnik's vineyard near the Masaryk Look-out

the ramparts into the other side of which are set the cottages in Golden Lane, the White Tower, the Powder Tower and other structures.

History

The slopes of the Stag Moat were previously predominantly bare or bore only low vegetation, and the Brusnice stream was lined with willows. From the second half of the 14th century secular and ecclesiastical owners of the land on the south–facing slopes began to plant grapevines. The land in the lower part of the moat was for the most part purchased by Ferdinand I. (1526–1564), when in the 1530's he began to lay out the Royal Garden. The moat as a whole came into royal hands in 1594, when Rudolf II bought most of what is now the Upper Stag Moat from Kryštof Popel of Lobkowicz as well as the remaining land to the east.

In the early years of the 17th century deer were introduced into the moat, under the care of a Keeper of the Harts and Willows. Hay for the deer was brought from the meadows of Zbraslav and elsewhere, as otherwise there was little for them to eat here in the summer. It was the responsibility of the Royal Building Office at Prague Castle to provide the deer with salt licks. After the Thirty Years' War the breeding of deer was reinstated. During his residence in Prague in 1723, Emperor Charles VI expressed displeasure at the high cost of breeding game in the moat, and in particular with the inconvenient shoot from the windows of the Spanish Hall, as the moat was deep and the sides particularly steep. In 1730 the herd was reduced to 25 animals. During the French Occupation of the 1740's foreign officers shot all of the remaining deer, which were never replaced – all that remains is of them is the name that they gave to the Stag Moat. In the second half of the 18th century the Stag Moat was the preserve of the Masters of the Hunt. During the Theresean reconstruction of the Castle the Powder Bridge was replaced by

a causeway (finished in 1771), through which a drain carried the Brusnice stream. It is from this time that the Stag Moat has been divided into Upper and Lower parts. From the end of the 18th century the Stag Moat passed through the hands of various enfeoffed owners, i.e. owners who, at the decision of the Court, could be required to surrender their property at any time. In 1831 the building of the Chotek road and the establishment of the Chotek Park led to the shortening of the Stag Moat. After arriving in Prague in 1848, the former Emperor Ferdinand V, called the Gracious, leased out part of the Upper Stag Moat with its glasshouses. One glasshouse was used exclusively for the rearing of camellias and rhododendrons. The Office of the Château Hetman bought back the Upper and Lower Stag Moats for 81,500 in Austrian gold, and then immediately leased the Upper Stag Moat back to the gardeners of Ferdinand V; the lessees were to cultivate the land in accordance with a plantation plan – fruit trees were to be among the most revered species, and without permission no trees or even shrubs were to be cut down. Access was restricted to well-mannered persons on a special ticket issued by the Office of the Château Hetman.

From the 1890's onwards the Municipality of Prague requested permission to drive a road and electric railway through the moat – all such requests were refused. Among those to speak out in opposition to the plan for an electric railway from Klárov to Hradčany across the Powder Bridge, along the Spanish Hall and through what is now the Bastion Garden to Hradčanské nám. were heir to the throne Ferdinand d'Este, the Viennese Central Commission for the Preservation of Structural and Artistic Monuments and cultured society as a whole. In consequence, the tram line was run over a newly created causeway and through a cutting along what is now ul. U Brusnice. Numerous dramatic events have also been played out along the Stag Moat, some at least of which can be mentioned here. In 1621 one of the participants in the Estates' Uprising, the lawyer Martin Fruwein, imprisoned in the

White Tower, unable to endure any longer his immeasurable suffering, jumped to his death in the moat fourteen days prior to the execution of 27 of the insurrection's leaders. His body lay at the foot of the moat for two days before being dismembered, the individual pieces subsequently exhibited around Prague... In May 1945, at the very end of the Second World War, the German occupiers murdered a number of mainly young people on the Powder Bridge; the site where their bodies were discovered is marked by a stone obelisk, and the victims' names are recalled on a plaque to the left in front of the access to the Powder Bridge embankment. In 1920 a bear pit was established in the Upper Stag Moat. From 1950 onwards, under the Communist regime, an extensive bunker was built beneath the Castle, access to which was from the base of the Lower Stag Moat. The joining of the two parts of the moat by a tunnel is the result of repeated consideration of the removal of the causeway; the newly-built pedestrian access was opened to the public in the 2001–2 season.

XI. THE CHOTEK PARK

The Chotek Park lies adjacent to the Royal Garden to the east, beyond the Renaissance Summer Palace that brings the latter to a close. It is open to the public all year.

Walk

The park is reached by a path leading along the east wall of the Royal Garden, and thence towards Letna by a footbridge over the Chotek road. It is interesting in particular for its mature trees and the original means by which it is joined to the Royal Garden and the panorama of the Summer Palace. Within the Chotek Park stands a monumental memorial to the writer Julius Zeyer, whose admirers began to campaign for it to be erected after his death in 1901, selecting this beautiful site for it. In the spring of 1902 a celebration was held in the Royal Garden and other adjoining gardens, the proceeds of which went to a society which had as its aim the creation of a memorial. The gentlemen's committee was headed by František Ladislav Rieger, and the lady's committee by Zdeňka Hlávková--Havelková. In 1904, the Supreme Hofmeister's Office in Vienna gave its agreement to the establishment of a memorial to a design by the sculptor Josef Maudr. Despite various delays, the society's work culminated in the ceremonial unveiling of the Julius Zeyer Memorial in 1913. An overflowing basin forms part of the Zeyer Memorial, close to which grow large Black Poplars *(Populus nigra)*.

The dominant feature of the park is Queen Anne's Summer Palace, in front of which stand two majestic, wonderfully tall plane trees *(Platanus hispanica)*. A group of birches can be admired in the eastern section, with undergrowth comprising rhododendrons and mahonias, while in the western section there is a group of oaks. The busy Chotek road with its tram lines is shaded mainly by maples, ashes, acacias and limes, with thick shrubbery composed

The pool by the Zeyer Memorial in Chotek Park

The Julius Zeyer Memorial in Chotek Park

THE RAMPART AND HARTIG GARDENS

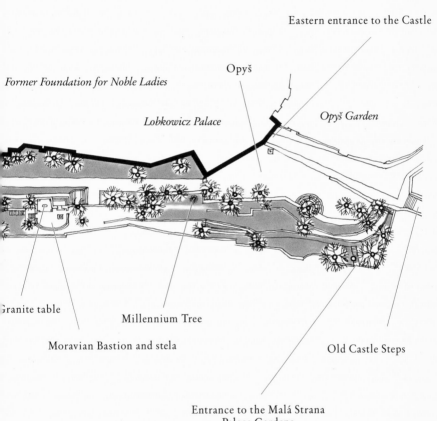

Eastern entrance to the Castle

Opyš

Former Foundation for Noble Ladies

Lobkowicz Palace

Opyš Garden

Granite table

Millennium Tree

Moravian Bastion and stela

Old Castle Steps

Entrance to the Malá Strana
Palace Gardens

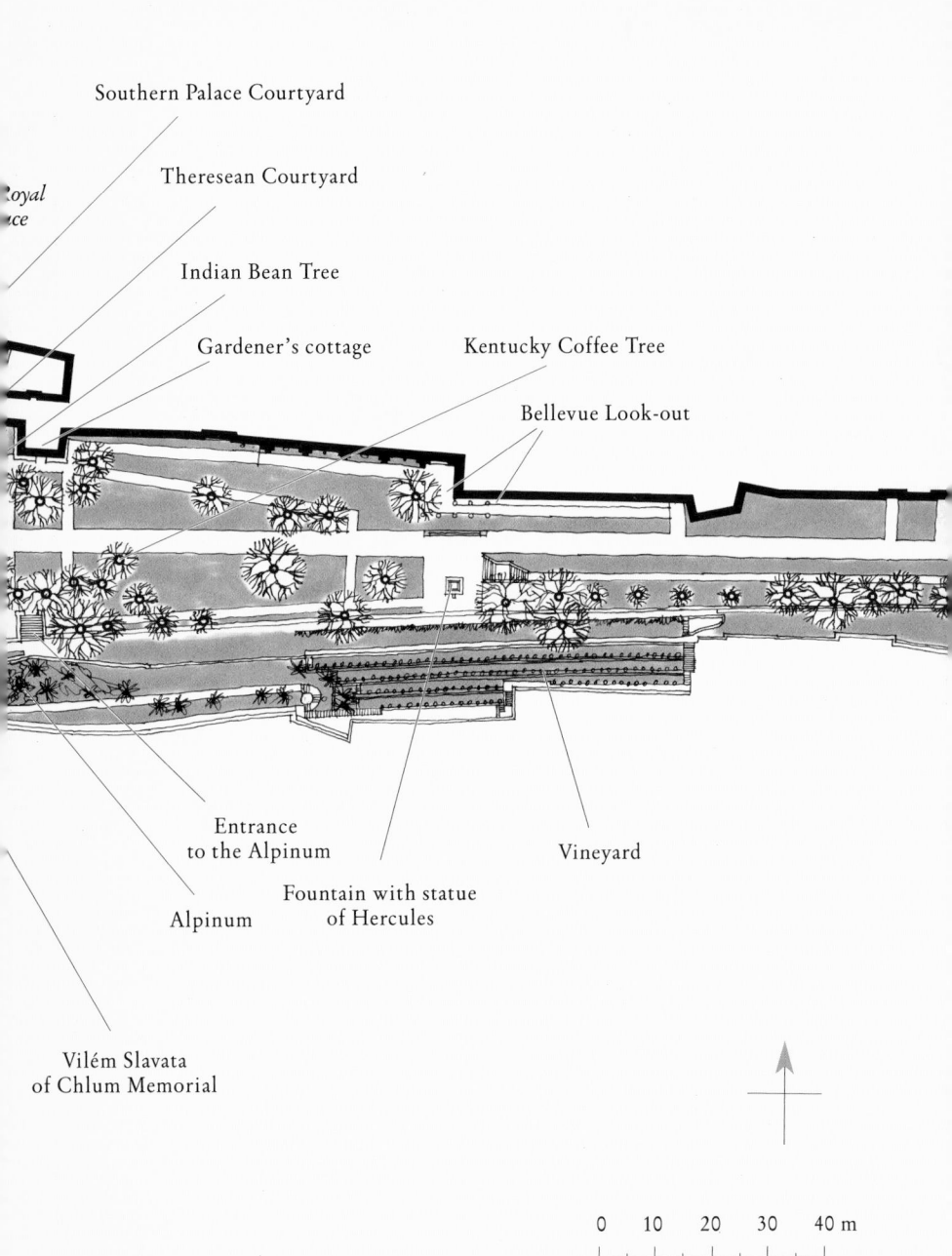

Southern Palace Courtyard

Theresean Courtyard

Indian Bean Tree

Gardener's cottage

Kentucky Coffee Tree

Bellevue Look-out

*Royal
ce*

Entrance
to the Alpinum

Vineyard

Fountain with statue
of Hercules

Alpinum

Vilém Slavata
of Chlum Memorial

0   10   20   30   40 m

predominantly of woodbine, snowberry, elder, meadowsweet, forsythia, mock orange, lilac, cherry etc. The relatively large grassy area in the spaces offers plentiful room for visitors to circulate or relax.

History

Chivalric tournaments and other court and noble games once took place in what is now the Chotek Park. In the 17th century this plot formed part of the economic hinterland of Prague Castle and was known as the Upper Wood Pen (the Lower being at Klárov). It was here that building timber and firewood were collected to meet the Castle's needs, while dried grass was collected in the ricks. In later centuries, too, this land served practical purposes, although it was still used occasionally for entertainment – such as the equestrian tournaments known as "carousels". Given the position of the Upper Wood Pen close to the walls, it often attracted the attention of the Military Commission. Thus, in the 1720's the Fortifications Commission pointed out that it would be necessary to build a new wall around the pen in conjunction with the building of the Písek (Brusko) Gate. A considerable part of the archive reports until the beginning of the 19th century then concerns the need for repairs to the perimeter and terrace walls.

Prior to the end of the 18th century the land was often leased out – for instance in 1779 it was leased by the Provincial Director of Building F. A. L. Herget, and subsequently by the Court Gardener and other staff of the Castle Building Office. Immediately below the Royal Summer Palace to the east lay a tilled field, to which a nursery was attached. This field too was leased by the Court Building Office, and then by officers of the artillery laboratory which from the end of the 18th century occupied the Royal Summer Palace. A fundamental change in the use of the area east of the Summer Palace came about during Count Karel Chotek's tenure (1826–1844) as head of the

81

Provincial government. Immediately after his ascent to this position, the new governor set about the modernisation of Prague, devoting himself to the construction of new lines of communication and attempting to beautify the city through the planting of trees and shrubbery. He first had the promenade along the city walls in the New Town repaired, and later – under an official directive issued in 1831 – had the Upper Wood Pen converted into the first urban, public park – the People's Garden. This park was somewhat larger than the Chotek Park of today, and reached close to the bastion – the agreement of the General Directorate of the Military was required for the changes. The park conversion was undertaken by the gardener of the Bubeneč enclosure, Josef Fuks; work was completed in just one year, at a cost of 5,131 in gold. Both the nobility and the citizenry contributed to the park both financially and through the donation of trees. The building of the new road that connected the Lesser Quarter to the Marian Ramparts via a hairpin bend followed. Hitherto it had been possible to reach the Písek Gate on the Marian Ramparts via a sunken road known as the 'Mouse hole', and old route that crossed a small bridge to link the gardens on both sides of the Chotek road. The Stag Moat, which had previously stretched as far as the cottages on the 'Mouse hole' was shortened to take account of the new road, and the Brusnice stream channelled into a new course through drains. The People's Garden opened to the public in 1841, and this important act by Karel Chotek is commemorated by its later having been renamed the Chotek Park. Various small entrepreneurs appeared who wished to build in the new park, such as the confectioner Koukal who wished to establish a restaurant here and the master baker Tägl who planned a shop for the sale of white baked goods; ultimately it was decided to erect an observatory here. The Court Building office officially gave over the Chotek Park to the use of the Prague municipality in 1859, albeit that major changes therein were to remain conditional on the agreement of the Castle administration, represented after 1860 by the Office of the Château

Hetman. The landscaping of the park at the end of the 19th century was designed by the then Director of Prague Parks and Gardens, František Thomayer (brother of the well-known doctor, Josef Thomayer). At the very beginning of the 20th century that section of the city wall preventing the direct continuation of the Chotek road to Dejvice was demolished. The Chotek Park lost those plots on which the original ramparts had stood and which were converted into building plots. Interesting structures appeared following the line of the earlier bastions – such as the original villa of the sculptor František Bílek.

After the establishment of the Czechoslovak Republic, a number of designs were drawn up for the alteration of the area between Letna and Hradčany, including the Chotek Park. Among the most important of these was the project by architect Josip Plečnik, which suggested the creation of a large pool in the middle of the park and rerouted the Chotek road over a curved flyover. Designs by the architect Pavel Janák are also known from the end of the 1930's, and a series of further studies were prepared by architects in the 1960's, at which point a new footbridge linking the Letna and Chotek Parks was built (designed by the architect Josef Fragner). The scenic pedestrian route thus created was intended to continue on past Prague Castle and Hradčany all the way to Petřín. Since 1998 a new footbridge, replacing that built in the 1960's, has led over the Chotek road; it was designed by the architect Bořek Šípek.

Changes in the political situation led in the 1990's to the resolution of the question of the property rights appurtenant to the Chotek Park; prior to this time it had been used and administered by the Public Greenery Administration of the City of Prague, while from 1992–96 it had come under the Prague 1 District Council. The cadastral record, however, showed ownership to lie in the "Czechoslovak State", and as the representative of its successor the Prague Castle Administration accepted oversight of the area on January 15th, 1997.

INDEX OF NAMES

85

Numbers in italics refer to figure captions

GLOSSARY OF TERMS

Alpinum – a natural or artificial rocky slope used for rearing mountain plants

balustrade – a row of small, usually rounded, pillars supporting a rail or coping

château hetman – an officer of the Crown charged with administering a major estate

giardinetto – an Italianate, small, formal garden of the Renaissance or Baroque period, with several smaller parts forming a pleasant whole

parterre – a formal arrangement of flower-beds, often on a terrace

pergola – a framework for climbing plants, more open than a trellis and often passing overhead

putto (pl. putti) – in Renaissance and Baroque art, a "cupid" figure, a small, plump, naked boy, often with wings.

sgraffito – Plaster decoration comprising incised patterns, the top coat being cut through to reveal a different colour beneath.

thermophilic – warmth loving

voliére – a large birdcage or aviary, set as a separate pavilion within the overall composition of the garden.

SELECT BIBLIOGRAPHY

Josip Plečnik – architekt Pražského hradu. Exhibition catalogue, Prague, 1996

Bašeová, Olga & Vilímková, Milada, 1991, Pražské zahrady. Prague

Chotěbor, Petr et al, 1993, Zahrady Pražského hradu. Prague

Lukeš, Zdeněk, 1996, Plečnikovy jižní zahrady Pražského hradu. Prague

Morávek, Jan, 1938, "Z počátků Královské zahrady", Umění XI pp530–536

Pacáková-Hošťálková, Božena et al., 1999, Zahrady a parky v Čechách, na Moravě a ve Slezsku, Prague

Procházka, Viktor, 1976, Zahrady Pražského hradu, Prague

Valena, Tomáš, 1991, "Plečnik's Garden at Hradčany: in search of the modern architectonic gardens of the 20th century", Architektov bilten 20, pp107–108, Ljubljana

Vávrová, Věra, 2001, "Prague Castle Gardens", in Encyclopedia of Gardens, History and Design vol. 3, pp1077–1081, Chicago & London

Vávrová, Věra & Ondřejová, Vítězslava, 2000, "Zahrady Pražského hradu" in Pacáková-Hošťálková, Božena et al., Pražské zahrady a parky, Prague

Wirth, Zdeněk, 1943, Pražské zahrady, Prague

87

CONTENTS

Prague Castle

Gardens and Parks

Published by the Prague Castle Administration
(Správa Pražského hradu)
Sponsored by the Office of the President of the Republic
Text: Věra Vávrová, Pavel Janeček
English translation: Alastair Millar
Photography: Zdeněk Thoma
Maps: Vojtěch Veverka
Editor: Hana Pešinová
Supervising Editor: Božena Pacáková, Pavel Janeček
Graphic design: Ivan Exner
Bound by Jiří Vašíček, Studio N.R.
Printed by PROTISK, České Budějovice

*Cover: an anonymous, mid-18th century plan of Prague Castle
and part of Hradčany,
from the Charles University Maps Collection*

First edition, Prague, 2002
ISBN 80–86 161–63–3